A Fortunate Drink

A Fortunate Drink

Tarot Through the Lens of Cocktails

Rose Raiser Jeavons
Emma Rose McClain

Crafted Co.

A FORTUNATE DRINK
Tarot Through the Lens of Cocktails

Published by Crafted Co.

Library of Congress Control Number: 2022945174

ISBN (hardcover): 9781662931383

THANK YOUs

SPIRIT HAUS OF AMHERST, MA
CHRISTOPH COX
CYNTHIA RAISER JEAVONS
LISHKA MCCLAIN
DREW DAILY

TABLE OF CONTENTS

INTRODUCTION 5

SOME THINGS TO KNOW... 6

MAJOR ARCANA 8

THE FOOL 10
THE MAGICIAN 12
THE HIGH PRIESTESS 14
THE EMPRESS 16
THE EMPEROR 18
THE HIEROPHANT 20
THE LOVERS 22
THE CHARIOT 24
STRENGTH 26
THE HERMIT 28
THE WHEEL OF FORTUNE 30
JUSTICE 32
THE HANGED MAN 34
DEATH 36
TEMPERANCE 38
THE DEVIL 40
THE TOWER 42
THE STAR 44
THE MOON 46
THE SUN 48
JUDGMENT 50
THE WORLD 52

PENTACLES	54	**WANDS**	114
THE ACE OF PENTACLES	56	THE ACE OF WANDS	116
THE TWO OF PENTACLES	58	THE TWO OF WANDS	118
THE THREE OF PENTACLES	60	THE THREE OF WANDS	120
THE FOUR OF PENTACLES	62	THE FOUR OF WANDS	122
THE FIVE OF PENTACLES	64	THE FIVE OF WANDS	124
THE SIX OF PENTACLES	66	THE SIX OF WANDS	126
THE SEVEN OF PENTACLES	68	THE SEVEN OF WANDS	128
THE EIGHT OF PENTACLES	70	THE EIGHT OF WANDS	130
THE NINE OF PENTACLES	72	THE NINE OF WANDS	132
THE TEN OF PENTACLES	74	THE TEN OF WANDS	134
THE PAGE OF PENTACLES	76	THE PAGE OF WANDS	136
THE KNIGHT OF PENTACLES	78	THE KNIGHT OF WANDS	138
THE QUEEN OF PENTACLES	80	THE QUEEN OF WANDS	140
THE KING OF PENTACLES	82	THE KING OF WANDS	142
SWORDS	84	**CUPS**	144
THE ACE OF SWORDS	86	THE ACE OF CUPS	146
THE TWO OF SWORDS	88	THE TWO OF CUPS	148
THE THREE OF SWORDS	90	THE THREE OF CUPS	150
THE FOUR OF SWORDS	92	THE FOUR OF CUPS	152
THE FIVE OF SWORDS	94	THE FIVE OF CUPS	154
THE SIX OF SWORDS	96	THE SIX OF CUPS	156
THE SEVEN OF SWORDS	98	THE SEVEN OF CUPS	158
THE EIGHT OF SWORDS	100	THE EIGHT OF CUPS	160
THE NINE OF SWORDS	102	THE NINE OF CUPS	162
THE TEN OF SWORDS	104	THE TEN OF CUPS	164
THE PAGE OF SWORDS	106	THE PAGE OF CUPS	166
THE KNIGHT OF SWORDS	108	THE KNIGHT OF CUPS	168
THE QUEEN OF SWORDS	110	THE QUEEN OF CUPS	170
THE KING OF SWORDS	112	THE KING OF CUPS	172

INTRODUCTION

In a divine pairing of mysticism and mixology, *The Fortunate Drink* brings together the emotions and intuition of Tarot and the fun and therapy of a well-crafted cocktail in the comfort of your own kitchen (or bubble bath, no judgment). Mix together, shake well, and presto! You have a guide to both the future and the depths of your liquor cabinet, simultaneously bringing the advice of Tarot to your life and possibly answering the question of what to do with that bottle of brandy you forgot you owned.

All seventy-eight Tarot cards are broken down, and their individual essence is distilled into an easy-to-follow cocktail recipe, perfect for whatever situation you find yourself in. The guidance given by each card sums up any moment of life with kindness, understanding, and a dose of humor and pours you the perfect drink for the situation. So, pull up the proverbial bar stool and learn a little of the unknown while sipping a cocktail crafted just for the occasion.

SOME THINGS
TO KNOW...

Rimming glasses is a pretty straightforward process. You start by getting two plates with a circumference at least as large as your glass. Then on one plate put honey, sugar syrup, or agave. Dip the rim of your glass into your sticking agent of choice, making sure the glass rim is completely covered. Next, pour your salt, sugar, or flower petals onto your other plate. Then place the glass rim in your mixture, rotating the glass as needed for even distribution. Once your glass is rimmed, add in any ice and then your pre-made drink.

To make simple syrup, start by putting 1 cup of water and 1 cup of sugar in a pan. White sugar is most commonly used because it doesn't have additional flavor or color, but you're welcome to experiment if you wish! Then bring this mixture to a boil, stirring to ensure that the sugar doesn't burn. Once the sugar has dissolved, take the mixture off the heat and allow it to cool. If you are making a flavored simple syrup, such as rose, you will add in a few tablespoons (2–4) of your herbs or citrus right after you turn off the heat. Then, place a lid on your pan to allow the herbs to infuse. For almost all syrups, boiling the plant material is not necessary, and it will lead to a loss of flavor and color.

Infusing booze is a very easy process. Start by finding a wide-mouthed jar with a lid. Then, fill the jar with your plant material (lemon slices, ginger, lavender, etc.), and pour your liquor of choice into the jar, making sure all your plant material is covered. Now store your infusion in a cool, dark place for a minimum of two weeks, although you'll get the best flavor if you let it infuse for six weeks or longer.

When choosing a garnish for your drink, always ensure what you're using is edible!

Some of our drinks suggest citrus twists. We recommend looking up a video online if you wish to execute this, as it is one of those things that is best shown instead of explained in text.

THE
MAJOR
ARCANA

These are the moments in our lives that should not be ignored, the events and people that will make lasting marks on who we are and who we will become. Each card in the Major Arcana has a distinct and unavoidable personality. These cards help to put a personification upon the weddings, funerals, and road trips that together create the soundtrack to our life. Each Major Arcana is the distilled essence of a role we will take on. These cards add weight to a reading and amplify themes that shouldn't be missed.

We are all complicated, created from an ever-growing tapestry of experience, every significant moment adding new aspects to our personalities. The star card may describe the friend who helped to heal long standing wounds, The Strength card might be the moment you stood up for what you believe despite the difficulties that barred your way, and let's face it, who doesn't have a little bit of Devil in them?

0
THE FOOL

Pour the following into a glass:

Ice
2 shots amaretto
Top with soda water

•

The Fool is the card of new beginnings and youthful dalliance. Blindly walking off a cliff in search of a new experience, The Fool is anything but wise. For me, the best instance of The Fool card manifesting into my life was the first time I ever drank to excess. There I was, leaning against a pink paper tablecloth on unsteady legs at my grandmother's 70th birthday party, sucking down yet another amaretto and soda, blindly unaware of what havoc was being done to my digestive system (oh boy, did I find out). I was happy as a clam in my blissful ignorance of the goodness of water and keeping track of my drink number.

Rose here, and I also have my own history of mixing foolish youth with amaretto. As a sixteen-year-old goody-two-shoes, a friend decided I should try to discover my drinking limits before going to college. Her suggestion for executing this was for me to take consecutive shots of amaretto and tequila, fourteen shots in total, if I remember correctly. If you're thinking that these flavor profiles wouldn't mix well, you'd be right, but believe me, it tasted a lot better going down than it did coming back up! This little event was my initiation into the world of drinking, leaving me with a bit more wisdom, a strong appreciation for water, and an experience I won't be repeating!

I
THE MAGICIAN

Add the following to a cocktail shaker:

Ice
1 shot gin
1 shot Aperol
3 shots grapefruit juice
Shake and serve

•

The Magician's energy is about creating the life of your dreams. Whether a grand scheme or minute detail, all you must do is assume it's already yours. This card depicts the Magician with each of the Minor Arcana suits (a wand, a pentacle, a sword, and a cup) at his disposal. However, perhaps the most essential detail is the infinity sign above his head. We are reminded that there are no limits except the ones we impose upon ourselves. We chose this delicious drink because it is both enchanting and refreshing, the perfect thing to sip while reveling in your divine power. Embrace your birthright to let life happen through you instead of to you. Your life is yours alone to manifest.

II
THE HIGH PRIESTESS

Add the following to a cocktail shaker:

Ice
2 shots mezcal
2 shots pomegranate juice
1/2 shot triple sec
Shake
Pour into a champagne bath glass
Garnish with pomegranate seeds if desired

•

Picture a woman dressed impeccably, sitting alone at a bar, with the type of silent contentment that can only come from inner mastery. The High Priestess trusts her intuition above all else, and her emotions are the key to the wisdom she holds. She has embraced herself, both shadow and light. Because of that, she wields a type of power that is often feared by others because of its strength and subtlety. This mezcal pomegranate martini embodies that intoxicating mystique of not only knowing the future, but also creating it.

III

THE EMPRESS

Pour the following into a glass after rimming:

Rim glass with sugar and rose petals
1 shot rose simple syrup
Top with champagne
A dash of Grand Marnier
Garnish with raspberries

.

The Empress is the card of The Divine Feminine. Depicted sitting upon a throne and in many renditions shown as pregnant, she is the ultimate creator. The influence she wields is entirely different than that of the Emperor, and she wouldn't want it any other way. She is striking in her gentleness, calm and patient in manner, and above all, confident in her unique understanding of the world. This rose champagne cocktail is a lovely way to imbibe in the potency of innate femininity and her many facets.

IV

THE EMPEROR

Add the following to your glass:

1 sugar cube
A few dashes Angostura Bitters
Crush together gently in your glass
2 shots of your favorite whiskey
A splash of water
Sweep the glass rim with an orange peel
Garnish with an orange twist

•

The Emperor perfectly embodies the Divine Masculine and the vital role he plays. Affectionately known as the "Daddy's Home" card by a favorite reader of mine, Victoria the Medium, this man is about to bring strength, stability, and maybe even a little smolder into your life. Instantly commanding respect, he will put anyone who confronts him in their place with little effort and go to any lengths to provide protection and peace of mind to those he loves. This classic drink is perfect for the simple yet mighty attitude that the Emperor exudes.

V

THE HIEROPHANT

Pour the following into a glass:

Ice
A few drops of food grade frankincense essential oil
2 shots gin
Tonic water
Garnish with fresh herbs if desired

.

As the masculine counterpart to The High Priestess, The Hierophant often represents structures of power in our lives. He signifies religion, politics, and our society as a whole. When this card appears in a reading, it may also be telling you that union or marriage is in your near future. We chose this frankincense gin and tonic as a nod to the use of frankincense in religious practices throughout history. Its mystical aroma and sought-after healing properties will signify the energy The Hierophant brings into our lives.

VI
THE LOVERS

Pour the following into a glass... or two!

2 shots bourbon
Honey to taste
Stir together until the honey is fully incorporated
Add ice
Garnish with raspberries

.

Who doesn't want to see The Lovers pop up in their Tarot reading? The timeless beauty of being in love will never lose its magic. This card speaks to each relationship's unspoken potential to keep the hearth of the honeymoon phase alight throughout every season of love. It also gently warns of the potential for codependency, addiction, and toxicity, as The Lovers card can easily become its sister card, The Devil. We chose this simple honey, bourbon, and raspberry cocktail as something you could drink with your beloved by the fireplace while snow falls outside or on a hot summer's night while watching the sun go down. Whatever season of love you might find yourself in, enjoy the hell out of it and drink up!

VII
THE CHARIOT

**Pour the following into a glass rimmed
with brown sugar:**

Ice
4 shots coffee (or more if desired)
Top with 2 shots Irish cream

•

Do you know those moments when everything finally falls
into place? Your crush asks you out, you win a scratch-off
ticket, and that bitch from work just got fired.... all in the
same day! We chose this iced Irish coffee to make those days
where everything goes right feel even better. The Chariot is
about victory but, more importantly, all the hard work and
patience that got you to this point. You chose to live as if you
already had the life you wanted, and guess what.... now you
do!

VIII

STRENGTH

Mix the following and then pour into a shot glass:

2 shots lemon and ginger-infused bourbon
Add honey
Take as a shot

•

Sometimes you're just fucking done, but you don't have the luxury of giving up. However life may be testing you, this card reminds you to find strength in unexpected places. Whether that may be a friend, this shot of bourbon, or, ideally, yourself, trust that you've got what it takes to tackle what's at hand. When you need liquid courage or a little fuel to keep the old engine going, this honey, lemon, ginger shot will help you feel a little extra lionhearted.

IX

THE HERMIT

Pour the following into a glass:

1 shot sage simple syrup
2 shots bourbon
A splash of water
Add ice
Stir
Add a smoking sage leaf if you'd like

•

Sometimes you just need to be alone. The Hermit wisely sees the benefit in doing his own thing, using this time to organize his thoughts and contemplate things that he finds intriguing. This smoky sage and bourbon cocktail should help you settle into your own company and find the simple joy in solitude.

X

THE WHEEL OF FORTUNE

Pour the following into a glass:

2 shots chilled grapefruit juice
Top with chilled champagne
Garnish with a sprig of thyme

•

The Wheel of Fortune appears when destiny is about to throw you a curveball, such as, a windfall of money, the romance of a lifetime, or perhaps a job offer that will take you across the globe. The winds of fate are ready to shift, and if the card appears upright, it will presumably be in your favor. The card of answered prayers and unexpected blessings is about to rock your world! So get excited, and make sure you have a bottle of bubbly on hand to celebrate with this grapefruit mimosa.

XI

JUSTICE

Add the following to a cocktail shaker:

2 shots straight cranberry juice
2 shots vodka
Shake with ice and serve

*sugared rim optional, depending on your mood

•

There are few feelings that compare to Justice being served in our lives. When someone has done you wrong and they get their "just desserts," the riotous glee one feels is unparalleled. We always get excited when the Justice card appears in a reading, because it indicates that balance is about to be restored. This unsweetened cranberry martini is strong and to the point. We leave you with the decision to either sugar-coat it or just take it straight.

XII
THE HANGED MAN

Rim a glass with brown sugar
Then fill your glass with ice and add the following:

1 shot vodka
1 shot dark rum
1 shot bourbon
2 shots lemon juice
1 shot simple syrup (more if desired)
Top off with iced Assam tea

•

The Hanged Man suggests that you need to suspend yourself for a little bit to gain clarity on a situation. Our take on this was to give you a drink that gets you so fucked up that everything makes sense for a little bit! After one of these bad boys, your problems just might solve themselves, or at least you'll get to forget about them for a few hours!

XIII

DEATH

Pour the following into a sugar-rimmed glass:

1 sugar cube, crushed
1 shot of absinthe
Top with champagne
Add a few dashes of cherry bitters

•

Although it is rare to find someone who is excited to have the Death card appear in their reading, this card is actually one of our personal favorites. Embodying Pluto, the planet of death and rebirth, it lets us know that a major transformation is afoot. We put a slight twist on Ernest Hemingway's favorite drink, "Death in the Afternoon," to let you embrace the freedom that a death of something can bring into your life. Remember with any ending there may be sadness, but there should also be celebration for all that is to come.

XIV

TEMPERANCE

Add the following to a glass:

1 shot lemon balm simple syrup
Fill half the glass with chilled Meyer lemonade
Top off with your favorite wheat beer

.

Temperance is reminding you to bring balance into your life.
Ruled by the fire sign Sagittarius, this card speaks of finding
a balance between our passions and practicality. If this card
comes up in a love or friendship reading, you should take it
as a sign that emotional balance might need to be restored.
This mild and delicious lemon balm shandy perfectly embodies Temperance energy. Fresh, bright, and simple, you
might just gain a new perspective after a few sips!

XV

THE DEVIL

Rim a glass with white sugar
Add the following to a cocktail shaker:

Ice
1 1/2 shots black vodka
6 shots black cherry juice
A few dashes of cherry bitters

Shake and serve in your sugar-rimmed glass

•

The Devil is our shadow side, the darker twin of The Lovers card. He exemplifies codependency, addiction, and self-indulgence. There are few moments in our lives when humoring our shadow side is recommended, but on those rare occasions where we give in to temptation and let our darker half have the reins, this black cherry martini might just be the right cocktail. The inky black vodka provides this drink with a dark elegance that would make even the most hedonistic of us nod in approval. So, break out your martini shakers and silk stockings, and pack your bags for a weekend away down in Dante's Inferno.

XVI

THE TOWER

Pour the following into a tall glass:

Ice
1 1/2 shots vodka
1 1/2 shots mezcal
A splash of sparkling water
Top with foamed egg white
Top with a lemon twist

●

Because we can't in good conscience tell you to drink a tall glass of vodka on the rocks, drink this instead! If you're having a so-called "Tower moment," this strong and stormy drink will help ease the stress you're going through. The Tower card indicates that you are experiencing (or are about to experience) a time of extreme upheaval. Although not always negative, change is often quite hard. This time, too, shall pass, and in all honesty, the only thing you can do is buckle up and get ready for a bumpy ride.

XVII

THE STAR

**Muddle your mint with 1 tablespoon of sugar
in the bottom of your glass, then add the following
to a cocktail shaker:**

*Ice
1 cup chilled mint tea
2 shots tequila
Shake and serve over ice*

•

The Star shows us the creative energy of emotional and spiritual healing. She is a gentle yet powerful force with the confidence to let the world bring her what she needs instead of trying to micromanage everything. If you are in this space in your life, or maybe if you are struggling to let go and ascend to this state of calm, mixing up this mint tea mojito might be just the thing. The mint tea is both calming and hydrating to assist in mental clarity, and the tequila adds that little bit of liquid courage for those of us who need a little help letting go of our earthly selves.

XVIII

THE MOON

Add the following to a glass of your choice:

2 shots strong juniper gin
1 shot juniper simple syrup
Top off with lavender tonic water
May be served over ice

•

The Moon symbolizes our intuition and subconscious mind, and it can also highlight doubts and fears we need to become comfortable with. Although Moon energy can feel daunting to sit with, learning to embrace it can bring a lot of wisdom and lasting peace to your life. This juniper lavender gin and tonic is a perfect drink to bring along in a flask on a midnight walk to clear your head, and its fresh yet mystical flavor will help you unwind and explore the unseen.

THE MOON.

XIX

THE SUN

Pop open your favorite bottle of champagne!

When life is going even better than expected, and you're happier than you can remember being in a long time, why not make things even better by popping open a bottle of champagne? As the happiest card in the deck, The Sun card is always welcome in any reading. When it appears, a very happy time in your life is just around the corner and you should enjoy every moment of it!

XX

JUDGMENT

Add the following to a cocktail shaker:

Ice
1/2 shot white rum
1 1/2 shots golden rum
1 shot dark rum
1 shot lime juice
1 teaspoon pineapple juice
1 teaspoon papaya juice
1 teaspoon superfine sugar
Shake and pour into a glass over ice
Pour 1/2 a shot of 151-proof rum on top, using a spoon

•

The judgment card suggests that we may be grappling with a big decision, that we are about to be reborn in a big way, or both! You may be having a bit of an identity crisis at the moment, afraid to let old parts of yourself go to allow space for new ones. Rest assured, you are not alone in this experience. Life is made up of many personal rebirths, and allowing them to happen is always in our best interest. So buck up, knock back this drink affectionally known as "The Zombie," and get ready to be reborn!

XXI

THE WORLD

A glass of your favorite hard cider or mead

The World is the card of ultimate fulfillment, to put it simply, you have the world in your hands. Work, life, and love are all at peace with one another and happiness is the byproduct of this harmony. So crack open a jug of cider and enjoy with those closest to you. You have gained inner peace and joy, so don't be afraid to celebrate it in whatever way best expresses the lightness in your heart. I always picture a garden, friends and family sharing a meal under the orchard canopy, but however complete wholeness is manifested for you, please go out and have a toast, you've earned it!

PENTACLES

Pentacles embody stability in its purest form. These cards show the grounded, stately forms of material comfort in all its different manifestations. When pentacles enter the conversation, they describe growth in one's professional life, finances, or the stability and warmth offered by a home. These cards are not for the impatient. They are representations of the slow growth that can take a lifetime to reach its full potential. Deeply connected with the earth element, pentacles grow in steady and mature seasons, slowly branching out into the world surrounding you. Just remember, it's worth the wait.

THE ACE OF PENTACLES

Add the following to a glass:

Ice
1 1/2 shots bourbon
1 shot Aperol
A squeeze of Meyer lemon
Top off with champagne

•

The Ace of Pentacles speaks of stable beginnings; this card exemplifies getting a grounded start in the right direction and having the patience to see things through. This start might be in the form of newfound financial stability, becoming part of a community, or maybe you just put a down payment on the house you've had your eye on for a while. If this is where you are, let us start by saying congratulations! There's still a lot of work ahead, but you know what you signed up for. Before you execute all the upcoming steps, sit back and enjoy this moment with an earthy and delicious cocktail.

THE TWO OF PENTACLES

Add the following to a cocktail shaker:

Ice
1 1/2 cups normal milk or not milk
(macadamia is our favorite)
1 splash maple syrup
1 splash rosewater
A little bit of vanilla extract
1 tbs matcha
2 shots gin
Shake and serve over ice

•

By any chance, do you have too much on your plate? The Two of Pentacles usually shows its face when we're juggling Way. Too. Much. We get it; sometimes everyone in your life has decided you're the best man for the job, and who could blame them? You probably are! That said, if you don't start saying no to some of them, you will have a nervous breakdown! Stop agreeing to work on the weekends, tell your sister she needs to grow up and start handling her own problems, and ask your hubby if he can watch the kids tonight. Then sit down with your calendar and this boozy latte to figure out which of your many obligations will have to go! We both know that you can't go on like this forever!

THE THREE OF PENTACLES

Pour the following over ice into a glass of your choice:

2 shots of your favorite dark rum
Top with your favorite cola

•

The Three of Pentacles is the card of creation and collaboration, filled with the kind of genius that can only come from late-night conversations with dear friends. When we're in this headspace, we imagine ourselves sitting in a bar or coffee shop going over plans for a new project. For evenings such as these, we're partial to a classic drink that never loses its charm, the rum and coke. It's simple, easy, and has just enough sugar and caffeine to keep the conversation flowing into the wee hours.

THE FOUR OF PENTACLES

Pour the following into a cocktail shaker:

2 shots rum
2 shots coconut cream
2 shots pineapple juice
1/2 shot grenadine
Shake and pour over crushed ice

.

Are you clinging too tightly to a particular outcome in life? If this card came up, you probably are! Whether it's a relationship, friendship, your material things, or all of the above, this cocktail will help you stop giving a fuck and make you live in the damn moment! Inspired by Gayle, also known as Jennifer Lawrence's rum-drunk alter ego, we invite you to throw caution to the wind and embrace the magic that happens when you finally let go. While Pentacles often ask us to ground ourselves, The Four of Pentacles serves as a reminder to temporarily detach from the areas of our lives that we have become obsessed with. Who knows? You might find that what you want comes naturally when you stop trying so hard!

THE FIVE OF PENTACLES

Add the following to a heat-tolerant glass:

2 shots Meyer lemon and ginger-infused bourbon
Honey to taste
1 shot lemon juice
Top off with hot water and stir

•

The Five of Pentacles speaks to feeling left out in the cold by life, by those most important to us, and by ourselves. We've all been there and know moments like these suck some major ass. While nothing but time and forgiveness will allow this hurt to lessen, we hope that this warm honey, lemon, and bourbon cocktail will make your heart feel a little less cold. Keep in mind that sometimes all you have to do to get out of the storm is choose to go inside.

THE SIX OF PENTACLES

Add the following to a cocktail shaker:

Ice
2 1/2 shots of gin or vodka
3/4 shot of dry vermouth
2 shots olive juice
Shake and serve with olives if desired

•

At its best, the Six of Pentacles is a card of equal give and take. Yet sadly, often, those that give the most receive mere bread crumbs in return. If you are guilty of constantly taking care of everyone around you (even when they don't deserve it), we suggest this super dirty martini to give back to yourself when you need to recharge. Put your feet up and let everyone handle their own shit for one evening!

THE SEVEN OF PENTACLES

Put the following things through a juicer:
*Or use your favorite green juice

1 apple
4 kale leaves
1 lemon
1 quarter-sized piece of fresh ginger
2 stalks of celery
1 sprig of mint
Add 2 shots of gin or vodka
Use fresh mint or extra veggies as your garnish

•

The Seven of Pentacles evokes the energy of patience. While sometimes frustrating to hear, things that take a bit of time often bring us the most value in life. We chose this delicious Green Juice Bloody Mary because it takes a bit of patience to make, but it's well worth the wait. Full of plants to help cleanse your liver... so you can fuck it up again. You'll love the fresh taste and the grounded buzz you get from this delicious drink.

THE EIGHT OF PENTACLES

**Rim a glass with brown sugar
Then add the following to a cocktail shaker:**

*Ice
Your favorite cold black coffee
2 shots of whiskey
(add milk and sugar if desired)
Shake and serve over ice in your rimmed glass*

•

Diligent work is often the ticket to our most fervent desires. The Eight of Pentacles tells you to keep your nose to the grindstone and have faith in the process. When we have a goal that requires a lot of tedious work, the only thing to do is stay focused and enjoy each step as much as possible. Whether it's finals week, the holiday season, or a book you've been working on for years, this delicious iced Irish coffee will keep you going once all the midnight oil has been burned.

THE NINE OF PENTACLES

Brew 1 cup black Assam tea with rose petals and allow it to cool. Meanwhile, rim a glass with white sugar and crushed rose petals (edible gold leaf optional). Then add the following to a cocktail shaker:

Ice
Cooled Assam tea
Sugar to taste or 1 shot rose simple syrup
2 shots of bourbon

Shake and pour over ice, garnish with
a rose bud if you like!

•

The Nine of Pentacles is grounded, happy, and utterly satisfied with herself. She knows what she deserves, and there's no chance in hell she will accept anything less. So turn on Baby Tate's "I AM" and start mixing up this super classy bourbon, rose, and Assam tea cocktail. Enjoy this beautiful time in life while it lasts. You're so radiant that you won't be able to keep the suitors away!

THE TEN OF PENTACLES

Add the following to a cocktail shaker:

Ice
1 shot mint syrup
2 shots bourbon

Shake and pour over ice, then garnish with fresh mint.

•

Every ten-card in the minor arcana signifies completion. After working through the other cards in the suit, this ten comes to us when we've held our vision and worked diligently to create the life we desire. The Ten of Pentacles depicts an older man surrounded by his loving family and material comforts. As a little inside joke, with questionable political correctness, we chose this classic "old white man drink" as a reminder to create whatever your Ten of Pentacles might look like instead of creating a life that others might expect for you. Once you mix up this mint julep, sit back, enjoy what your hard work has yielded, and give society the middle finger.

THE PAGE OF PENTACLES

**Rim glass with sugar, then add the following
to a cocktail shaker:**

*Ice
2 shots cognac
1/2 shot Grand Marnier
1 shot ginger simple syrup
1 shot lemon juice*

Shake and serve with a lemon twist!

•

While Pages are notorious for their immaturity, The Page of Pentacles is perhaps the most endearing of the four suits. Although he lacks experience, he takes time to learn instead of rushing into situations. The Page of Pentacles may enter your life when you start something new that will take a lot of time and patience to master. Your best bet is to humbly admit what you don't yet know and seek guidance from those who do. This ginger sidecar holds youthful yet grounded energy that will give you a much-needed break from all your hard work.

THE KNIGHT OF PENTACLES

**Rim glass with sugar, then add the following
to a cocktail shaker:**

Ice
2 shots whiskey
1/2 shot Grand Marnier
1 shot sage simple syrup
1 shot lemon juice

Shake and serve!

•

The Knight of Pentacles can often be someone coming into our lives to offer stability. Whether this is a friend, a family member, or a romantic interest, you can rest assured that this individual is in it for the long haul. They are just one of those people who always show up when you need them. As the slowest-moving knight in the four suits, you may sometimes feel frustrated by their seemingly sluggish and over-planned approach to life. Do your best to appreciate the wisdom and strength of those with this temperament. This sage sidecar is a perfect drink to share with whomever the Knight of Pentacles in your life might be; its smoky yet sweet taste can be easily savored throughout those late-night conversations.

THE QUEEN OF PENTACLES

**Brew a cup of English breakfast tea and
allow it to cool. Rim a glass with sugar, then add
the following to a cocktail shaker:**

Ice
2 shots bourbon
1 shot chamomile simple syrup
1 cup cooled English breakfast tea
1 shot Meyer lemon juice

**Shake, pour over ice, and garnish
with chamomile blossoms**

•

The Queen of Pentacles holds remarkably powerful yet quiet energy. She is generous, kind, and wise, taking her time to discern what decisions to make to ensure a positive outcome for all. This Queen is perceived as always having her shit together. With this subtly energizing yet surprisingly strong chamomile, English breakfast tea, and bourbon cocktail, you'll feel like life is right where you want it to be.

THE KING OF PENTACLES

Pour the following into a glass over ice:

2 shots scotch
1 shot lemon verbena simple syrup
Top off with club soda

•

The King of Pentacles is remarkably grounded while also having a soft spot for high-quality material things. This King will always show up when you need him, ready to give good advice and lend a listening ear. This scotch and lemon verbena drink is mature and luxurious, so take your time sipping it and listen to some Chris Stapleton if you want to elevate the experience.

SWORDS

The suit of intellect and truth, these cards symbolize the mind with its many facets and trials. Swords are deeply linked with the element of air, fresh and clean but also biting and sometimes destructive. The swords can be cold and aloof at times, but they are nonetheless a symbol of strength in the form of mental clarity and directness. Swords represent the force and ferocity of will needed to command logic. Cloaked in a foreboding feeling, they can express the fears and doubts of dwelling in the mind instead of feeling with one's emotions and heart.

THE ACE OF SWORDS

Add the following to a cocktail shaker:

Ice
1/2 shot absinthe
1 shot gin
1 shot Lillet Blanc
1 shot lemon juice
1 shot Cointreau

Shake and pour into a glass, adding an orange twist to garnish.

•

Have you ever had an old friend call you out of the blue to confess that they've been in love with you for years? This unexpected and direct communication is a perfect example of The Ace of Swords. We chose "The Corpse Reviver" for this card because whatever honest communication is coming your way may bring something or someone back into your life that you considered to be long gone. Buck up for what's to come because this is a case where honesty is undoubtedly the best policy.

THE TWO OF SWORDS

Add the following to a glass:

2 fingers of rye whiskey
Garnish with a thin slice of lemon

•

Sometimes we have to make a decision, and the answer is not coming as effortlessly as we might like. If this is the case for you, you might be in a Two of Swords mentality. When the Two of Swords is ruling your life, you may feel paralyzed by the choice at hand. Being trapped between two prospects can be unpleasant, but more often than not, it leads to growth. May we suggest taking a walk and a deep inhale before you pour yourself a simple glass of rye whiskey and lemon to ease the upcoming choice?

THE THREE OF SWORDS

If the image on the card didn't make this abundantly obvious, this is the card of heartbreak. It is a rare person who has never had their heart broken (and to be perfectly honest, we don't trust them), but even so, no one can pretend it's pleasant. If you are in the throes of the Three of Swords, then we would have to recommend the following course of action:

Step one: pour approximately two fingers
of scotch into a glass
Step two: draw a bath
Step three: drink said scotch
Step four: call a friend
Step five: drink water
(not from the bath, we are all adults here)
Step six: another finger of scotch
(repeat as necessary)

THE FOUR OF SWORDS

Make a cup of your favorite hot chocolate, we suggest going for a European-inspired recipe.

Then mix :
1 cup of whipped cream
1/2 shot bourbon
a splash of vanilla extract and 1 tsp maple syrup
whisk until it makes stiff peaks.

Pour your hot chocolate into a glass
Add 1 shot of whiskey
Top with your spiked whipped cream

.

The Four of Swords is the card of calm and logical contemplation. Have you ever had one of those moments when you're relaxed, at peace, and planning your next move in life? Maybe you're sitting back in your room listening to some records and casually looking at graduate schools, or perhaps you're at the kitchen table flipping through house listings for the future. Regardless of the details, you aren't ready to make a decision, but you are enjoying the peaceful contemplation of your future. This time might be perfect for a personal favorite: a warm cup of whiskey-laced hot cocoa with some bourbon whipped cream to top it off.

THE FIVE OF SWORDS

Add the following to a glass:

2 1/2 shots gin
1 shot lemon juice
1 shot lavender simple syrup
Stir
Top off with sparkling water
Garnish with a lemon slice

•

The Five of Swords depicts a man collecting swords from the ground after a battle. When you are in a Five of Swords headspace, you're having difficulty letting go of past troubles. You might be holding a grudge that has long since outlived its purpose or wallowing in the pain of a wrong that no longer serves you. We've all been there, but we know from personal experience that it is time to let go. The lavender in this lemon lavender gin fizz will help to calm your nerves and let you experience the sparkling joy that is sure to be in your future.

THE SIX OF SWORDS

Pour the following over ice:

2 shots Aperol
1 shot sparkling water
Stir
Top with sparkling rosé

•

Sometimes called the Refugee card, The Six of Swords illustrates moving toward calmer waters. It's a time to stop dwelling on past horrors and embark on a new voyage. Moving on is not without heartache, but it's also one of life's most potent remedies. Aperol spritzers are classic, classy, and sunny in flavor. This drink will help put you in an optimistic and content mood for your journey, whether emotional, spiritual, or even as tangible as a move to a new place.

THE SEVEN OF SWORDS

**Rim a glass with flakey sea salt and then
add the following to a cocktail shaker:**

Ice
2 1/2 shots mezcal
1 shot lime juice

Shake and pour into your glass

•

Plain and simple, The Seven of Swords is the card of be-
trayal. Disloyalty is an experience shared by nearly everyone. Whether the backstabbed or the backstabber, you can
probably conjure that pit-of-your-stomach feeling that goes
along with such situations. Although very uncomfortable,
these moments can positively define us if we actually learn
from them. This mezcal martini is not for the faint of heart,
but it might be just what you need if you're going through
hell right now. Often, these periods are met with a barrage
of tears, and the salted rim of the glass accompanies bitter
disappointment and guilt.

THE EIGHT OF SWORDS

Add the following to a cocktail shaker:

Ice
3/4 shot orange juice
3/4 shot brandy
3/4 shot whiskey
3/4 shot sweet vermouth

Shake and serve over ice, adding an orange twist to garnish.

•

The Eight of Swords is the Victim card. You have bound yourself up in life and have played the pity card for too long. Let's face it; nobody likes that guy. So, don't waste your life tied up in knots over your problems; give yourself a swift kick in the ass and get moving. This drink is sweet and strong, so even if the orange doesn't sweeten your day, the whiskey will send some liquid courage racing down your throat to help you break free of your own emotions.

THE NINE OF SWORDS

Brew a strong cup of chamomile tea
Add honey to taste
Finish by adding a shot or two of your favorite whiskey

•

This card carries the horrors and fears of nightmares and is filled with anxiety. Sometimes the world around us becomes plagued with the monsters of our minds, and banishing them can seem like an insurmountable task. Remember that you're not alone, and conquering your fears is only as difficult as waking up. When you find yourself lost between reality and the shadows of your subconscious, consider a cup of chamomile and honey for your shaking nerves. If you feel that liquor would help to steady your shaking hands, then a shot of your favorite whiskey in the mixture might be just the thing.

THE TEN OF SWORDS

Have 2 glasses of water (you'll thank us in the morning), and then add the following to a cocktail shaker:

Ice
1 1/2 shots vodka
1 1/2 shots apple liquor
1 shot lemon juice

Shake and serve

•

You drink this when your significant other cheated with your best friend, you got fired from your job, your grandpa died, and the neighbor shot your dog... all in the same week. The Ten of Swords is the completion of a harrowing cycle. This sour apple martini is perfect for when you want to suck on the sickeningly sweet taste of bitter disappointment. After you've wallowed in your pain for the appropriate amount of time, let the swords fall free from your back and get ready to watch the sunrise. Don't worry; there's an ace in your future.

THE PAGE OF SWORDS

Add the following to a cocktail shaker:

Ice
1 shot vodka
1 shot rum
2 shots blue pea flower tea
A squeeze of lemon juice
2 shots coconut cream
1 shot simple syrup

Shake and serve!

•

The Page of Swords is an intriguing card in that, on the one hand, he is intelligent and full of new ideas. Yet, on the other, he is rather immature and routinely overestimates his abilities. This tropical mix of coconut and rum is potently bright but, most importantly, young. Sometimes, it's best to be mature, sit back calmly, and do the right thing, but occasionally, you just want to have a little party and enjoy yourself.

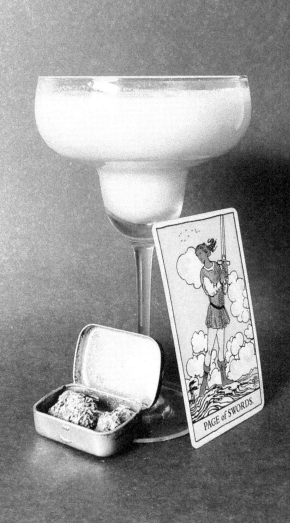

THE KNIGHT OF SWORDS

Pour the following into a glass over ice:

2 shots gin
1/2 shot lime juice
Top with tonic water
Serve with a lime twist

•

The Knight of Swords, though still young, is brilliant with a mind as sharp as the point of his blade. When you are the knight, you have the potential, unlike the page, to focus that youthful zeal on your endeavors. By utilizing the raw energy coursing through you, you have the potential to charge forward in life. The good old-fashioned gin and tonic sets the mood for a strong but not stingy chapter of life.

THE QUEEN OF SWORDS

Pour the following into a cocktail shaker:

Ice
1/2 shot French vermouth
1 shot mezcal
1/2 shot absinthe

**Shake and serve over ice, garnish with
a fresh sprig of mint**

•

Independent is the first word that comes to mind for The Queen of Swords, direct even to the point of brutality, the embodiment of unbiased judgment. This mezcal fascinator is like The Queen herself, assertive but not unfeminine. It will hit your tongue with sharp lashes of flavor and the hint of a burn, just like the stinging words that The Queen herself bestows upon her subjects when they deserve it.

THE KING OF SWORDS

Add the following to a cocktail shaker:

Ice
2 shots gin
2 shots Meyer lemon juice
Meyer lemon zest

Shake and serve over ice

•

The King of Swords is the epitome of mental clarity, truth, and drive. Happy to assert himself in any situation, he is in no way afraid to come across as harsh. If you want him to crack a smile, you need only mention books, the art of debate, or anything that furthers his pursuit of the intellectual. Gin and lemon, not unlike The King, are sharp, but if you give them a moment, they become more nuanced. Cutting, with more than a little bite to it, we expect this will help to solidify The King's energy into your spirit or perhaps fuel what is already there.

WANDS

The cards responsible for reflecting life's fire-in-the-belly, Wands are moments of unbridled passion, hot blood, and the draw of the physical. Due to the rash nature of Wands, they can spark difficulties from lack of forethought and contemplation. This absence of solidity can result in unreliability, but this is tempered by the strength of feeling these cards hold. Someone in this phase of life will fight for the ones they love with every ounce of their being.

THE ACE OF WANDS

Add the following to a glass with 2–3 ice cubes:

3 shots grapefruit Italian soda
2 shots vodka or gin
Top with Prosecco
Garnish with a lemon twist

.

This pretty pink drink is cigarettes after sex in liquid form, a celebration with a sensual twist. Sometimes, you must lean back and enjoy whatever small pleasures one has just experienced. This drink is sweet, smooth, and strong like any good lover. The Ace of Wands is a card of new beginnings and growth, making this the perfect drink for after your first night with a new person.

THE TWO OF WANDS

Pour the following over ice:

1 shot gin
1/2 shot elderflower liquor
1 1/2 shots absinthe
Stir
Top with sparkling water
Add a sprig of thyme to garnish

•

Sometimes we all need a little help when trying to tap into our creative potential; the Two of Wands wants to help spark discovery and inspiration. This potent and botanical cocktail helps to open the potential lurking within. The absinthe in this drink might just help you to look at the world around you with a little bit of an added glow. So, when you're sitting on the floor trying to ignite some shred of inspiration, consider going on a walk, whipping up this refreshment... or maybe both.

THE THREE OF WANDS

Add the following to a glass filled with ice:

1 1/2 shots Aperol
3/4 shot sparkling water or club soda
Top with Prosecco
Garnish with a fresh sprig of thyme

•

Take this as a sign to stop worrying and just be patient. The Three of Wands is the card of waiting for your ship to come in. However tempting it is to focus on and intently stare at your wishes, willing them to come your way, on occasion, you simply need to sit back and not watch the pot boil. This Aperol Spritz embodies the bubbling anticipation welling up in your chest and the slightly bitter tang of waiting. Who knows? All you might need is just a little more thyme.

THE FOUR OF WANDS

Add the following to a glass:

1 1/2 shots gin
1 shot freshly squeezed lemon juice
1 shot hibiscus simple syrup
Top of with champagne
Garnish with a lemon twist

•

The card of union, joy, and quite conceivably a wedding, if The Four of Wands falls into your lap, get ready to party! When celebrating the happiest day of your life, whether or not we are talking about traditional marriage, you may want to consider the refreshing and sparkling flavors of this hibiscus French 75. As you dance, hug, and kiss your way out into the next chapter of your life, this drink will send you on your way with some antioxidants for health and some champagne bubbles for the elation we're all feeling.

THE FIVE OF WANDS

Pour into a shot glass in this order, using the back of a spoon for a layering effect:

1 shot coffee liquor
1 shot Irish cream
1 shot Grand Marnier

•

The card of conflict and warring passions, sometimes the fires of passion get out of control and explode into a full kaleidoscope of pyrotechnics. This classic B52 shooter hits your palate with intense flavors and just a touch of violence. The B52 plane did a lot of damage in the second World War, and this drink, like its namesake, ought to do a little damage. So if you're feeling a smidge rebellious and like you need to let your more volatile side have a moment in the sun, the B52 will likely hit the spot.

THE SIX OF WANDS

Pour the following into a glass over crushed ice:

1 shot mint simple syrup
2 shots white rum
Stir
Top with Prosecco
Garnish with fresh mint and lime

•

Hopefully, you're a fan of public recognition, because it's about to come your way! Maybe you're up for a promotion, or your hard work has been paying off with some good old-fashioned "attaboys" from those around you. When you're celebrating with a drink and an evening of casual reverie, a twist on the traditional mojito sets the night off just the right way. Allow a few laughs with your friends and co-workers, and the sweet but tangy twist of lime on your tongue refresh you for the subsequent victory in your future.

THE SEVEN OF WANDS

Pour the following into a cocktail shaker:

Ice
1 shot vermouth
1 shot dry gin
1 shot Campari
Shake and serve over ice, garnishing with an orange twist

.

We have all had to stand up for something at one time or another, and The Seven of Wands is a prime example. This card depicts an individual wielding one wand against six other unsupported ones. Occasionally we have to go out on a limb and experience the challenge of conflicts and resolution on our own. This card can also show that you are fighting with yourself; in that case, you need to knock it off! This cocktail is meant to be sipped as you contemplate how to bring balance and harmony back into your sphere, whether that's by showing those around you that you are not afraid to stand up for your beliefs or by taking a moment to reconcile those beliefs within the walls of your own chest.

THE EIGHT OF WANDS

Pour the following into a glass:

1 shot triple sec
1/2 shot of ginger juice
1 1/2 shots high-proof vodka (if the alcohol percent
is too low it won't light)
light on fire
*Please blow out before drinking!!!

•

When the world moves fast, and you want to move with it, this is the drink for you. The Eight of Wands is like drinking out of a firehose and loving every drop. Since this is a cocktail book and we can't in good conscience recommend you visit your local frat house to do a keg stand, we will have to suggest this flaming ginger and vodka concoction that leaves both the heart and taste buds sparking. Be safe, drink water, and enjoy the ride for what it is: When you're in an Eight of Wands place in your life, it's guaranteed to be a rollercoaster.

*We are not responsible for any accident or injury resulting from this drink.

THE NINE OF WANDS

Have a glass of red wine or two
Call a friend
Go get a pedicure
Regroup

•

All wounded warriors need time to heal after battle. When your faith has been tested for what feels like the last time, take a moment to regroup and get your boots again on solid ground. Whether a romantic failure, a family difficulty, or maybe the world is generally getting the best of you. Sometimes it's just not the juncture for complicated or experimental cocktails, and the best thing we can do is revert to a classic. Pour yourself a glass of your favorite red, find a couch, and just take a break. Before you know it, that red wine will be replaced with champagne raised in a toast.

THE TEN OF WANDS

A pour of your favorite brandy

•

It's prudent to remember that the load of life can't all be carried in one go like your bags of groceries from the car. The Ten of Wands speaks of the burdens, hard work, and responsibilities that slowly eat away at our will to live. When you find yourself here, take a half hour, put your feet up, and pour yourself a nice glass of your finest brandy. Let this strong but flavorful liquor slide down your throat and help to wash away some of the stresses of the day.

THE PAGE OF WANDS

Whiskey sour jello shot
1 packet unflavored gelatin
1 cup boiling water
1/2 cup whiskey
1/4 cup lemon juice
1/4 cup simple syrup

Stir gelatin into water
Add whiskey, lemon juice, and simple syrup
Pour into shot glasses
Allow to chill for at least 2 hours or until solidified

•

This young, free spirit is amid discovery, probably not through measured, scholarly methods, but rather through the slightly more unpredictable (but infinitely more fun) process of trial and error. If you have ever been to spring break or turned 21, then you or one of your friends has probably been the Page of Wands. There isn't any drink, but the good ol' jello shot to exemplify this stage of development. So, without further ado, leave your car keys at home and see where the night takes you.

*If you have any issues with your gelatin solidifying, try adding less whiskey, lemon juice, and simple syrup.

THE KNIGHT OF WANDS

Flaming Fireball shot
Pretty self-explanatory
Pour a shot of Fireball
Carefully light it on fire
PLEASE blow this out before drinking!!

·

The Knight of Wands charges into life without glancing over his shoulder or considering the consequences of his desires. When you're The Knight of Wands, you're ready to gallop full speed ahead toward your target. Sometimes this is a person, a thing, or a really good time, but whatever lands as the apple of your eye, you are sure to chase after it enthusiastically. A flaming Fireball shot will fuel the passions of the naturally haphazard or ignite rebellion in even the most tempered souls.

*We are not responsible for any accident or injury resulting from this drink.

THE QUEEN OF WANDS

Pour the following into a bowl or large mason jar and allow it to sit in the fridge overnight. Make sure your bowl is tightly covered or that your jar has a lid!

1 bottle of sweet white wine
4 peaches, sliced
1 small container of raspberries or blackberries
Add sugar if desired
1 cup of brandy

•

This Queen is the social butterfly; she is happy, confident, commands attention, thrives in the spotlight, and is occasionally referred to as the third party card (wink wink). For this beautiful lady, a classic sangria would appear the logical choice, but it doesn't truly capture the experimentation and freedom of this Queen. So, to honor this part of yourself, a white sangria dripping with peaches would fit the bill perfectly.

THE KING OF WANDS

Pour the following into a glass over ice:

1/2 shot absinthe
2 ounces mezcal
1 ounce St. Elizabeth allspice dram
2 dashes Angostura bitters
Garnish with a rosemary sprig

•

He is a born leader, rugged and willful, with more than a pinch of impulsiveness. He meets the pursuit of his most fervent desires with a sense of humor and unparalleled resolve. To this King, absinthe and mezcal are savored with a sense of pride rather than pain. So mix yourself up a glass and relish in your innumerable victories and inexhaustible resilience.

CUPS

Cups are the vessels of emotion, holding the joy, fear, and love in our lives. They are the bridging force between the swiftness and biting edge of swords and the slow stability of the pentacles. These cards spill out their contents into our daily existence, giving emotional gravity to the moments we live. Cups may also represent offers and opportunities, especially in romance and other emotionally driven parts of life. Cups are precisely like the feelings they contain: strong, mature, and significant while also unpredictable and volatile. Closely connected to water, they personify the fluidity of our emotional lives and sometimes a few tears.

THE ACE OF CUPS

Rim a glass with sugar, then add the following to the glass:

1 shot elderflower cordial
Top off with champagne

•

The Ace of Cups means you are about to have a new emotional beginning, capturing the childlike nostalgia of falling in love with someone or something new. Whenever this golden moment happens in life, we have the beautiful ability to forget the pain of past loves lost and dive headfirst into this fresh opportunity. We came up with this champagne and elderflower cocktail with the image of it being sipped at a New Year's Eve party. Like the Ace of Cups, New Year's Eve holds so much excitement, potential, and hope for what is to come. Cheers to new beginnings, and may you have someone to kiss at midnight!

THE TWO OF CUPS

Add the following to a blender:

Ice
1 1/2 shots white rum
1 shot strawberry rhubarb simple syrup
(rhubarb must be fully cooked!)
3/4 shot fresh lime juice

Blend and serve with a slice of lime

•

The Two of Cups can signify a romantic relationship or a friendship that means the absolute world to you. This person might be new in your life, or they might be someone you've known for years. Either way, the Two of Cups in a reading suggests that your bond is about to deepen. We chose this strawberry rhubarb daiquiri to reflect the joyful yet nuanced feeling that goes along with this card. We suggest making a pitcher, grabbing two cups, and sharing it with your other half.

THE THREE OF CUPS

Add the following to a blender:

Ice
2 cups frozen pineapple
2 tablespoons honey
2 shots lime juice
1/2 cup tequila
1 tablespoon triple sec
Blend

Serve with a salted or sugared rim

•

This card is all about celebrating, and more specifically... drinking with friends. The Three of Cups lets you know it's time to let loose, embrace your favorite vice (within reason), and cherish the people you have around you. This frozen pineapple margarita is the perfect drink to start the night off right. Remember to keep the water flowing along with the margaritas, people!! As much fun as this is now, the sheets your mom just bought you for your dorm don't need puke on them!

THE FOUR OF CUPS

Add the following to a cocktail shaker:

Ice
1 cup tomato juice
2 shots vodka
The juice from 1 Meyer lemon
2 dashes of your favorite hot sauce
Pepper if desired

Shake and serve, garnish with celery and a slice of lemon

•

Affectionately known as the "take the fucking cup dude" card, The Four of Cups shows someone hesitant to take an offer from the divine. The three cups in front of them signify previous cups they have been offered, all of which have yielded nothing. However, the fourth cup likely holds what they've been looking for all along. This card might be the offer of a job, a relationship, or your friend trying to get you to down a hangover cure after you went too hard with the frozen pineapple margaritas last night. We chose this take on a bloody Mary because of its standing in the hangover cure hall of fame. Surprisingly delicious, it is just the ticket after too many sugary drinks. We only have one thing left to say: take the fucking cup, dude!

THE FIVE OF CUPS

Add the following to a heat-compatible glass:

1 tablespoon salted butter
2 shots dark rum
2 teaspoons fresh grated ginger
1 tablespoon honey
Top off with hot water

**Stir until butter and honey are fully dissolved,
balance flavors as necessary**

•

If you ever heard the saying "no use crying over spilt milk," you understand The Five of Cups. It's the temptation to spend your time focusing on the three cups spilled rather than being grateful for the two still brimming with possibility. When difficulty and loss knock you about, it's easy to feel the pain of what is lost. If you sense yourself falling into this age-old trap, a cup or two of hot buttered rum might do the trick in helping you to remember to bask in the warmth of the good rather than the sticky mess of what is gone.

THE SIX OF CUPS

Add the following to a blender:

4 large scoops vanilla bean ice cream
1 shot espresso
2 shots bourbon
1/4 cup whole milk
Blend until smooth
Top with boozy whipped cream
(see recipe from The Four of Swords)

•

One of my favorite cards, The Six of Cups, holds a meaning of those friends in our lives that make us feel eternally youthful. This milkshake will always make me think of a dear friend whose refusal to grow up is contagious, and for whom I invented this drink in the first place. The nature of The Six of Cups speaks of reconciliation with parts of ourselves we may have lost along the way, as well as being reunited with people we've had to love from afar for too long.

THE SEVEN OF CUPS

Add a 1/4–1/2 shot of each to a tall glass over ice:
tequila
mezcal
vodka
gin
elderflower liquor
white rum
limoncello
*Top with champagne or sparkling water

•

Affectionately known as "The Seven Wonders," this monstrosity of a drink was, not surprisingly, the brainchild of a late-night drunken conversation. The Seven of Cups is often described as a card of clouded judgment, substances, and illusion. While all these things are important aspects of its meaning, it is also a potent card of manifestation. Each cup represents your dreams around a specific part of your life: love, power, wealth, etc. I invite you to let go and allow yourself to realize what you need in life to feel fulfilled. When properly harnessed, Seven of Cups power can hold a euphoria that can only come from realizing your dreams. Mix up this fucker, put on Fleetwood Mac's classic "Seven Wonders," and get ready for a wild night!

**P.S. PLEASE STAY HYDRATED while drinking this!!!

THE EIGHT OF CUPS

Add the following to a cocktail shaker:

Ice
2 shots rye
1 shot sweet vermouth
A few dashes orange bitters

**Shake and serve over ice, garnishing
with an orange twist**

•

When we think of Eight of Cups energy, the song "What's Up" by 4 Non-Blondes comes to mind immediately. It's the feeling of being disillusioned with a situation you've found yourself in and what happens when you decide it's time to walk away. Though never an easy call to make, sometimes it's the only one you're left with. This simple rye Manhattan packs just the right amount of punch to get your ass out the door and heading toward better things.

THE NINE OF CUPS

A shot of Irish whiskey and a beer

·

When The Nine of Cups shows up, one of your wishes is about to be fulfilled. A welcome card to get in any reading, something you've been very emotionally invested in is finally showing up. This card could also be letting you know that you may be getting a drunk call from someone with a lot of feelings for you! We chose an Irish whiskey and your favorite beer for this card because it's a classic way to celebrate. You've waited, you've put in the work, and now it's time to enjoy the hell out of this long-awaited moment.

THE TEN OF CUPS

**Pour one bottle of red wine into a pan
and add the following:**

*2 tablespoons mulling spices
1 orange peel
2 cups of sugar (more if desired)
Simmer with a lid for 10 minutes
Remove from the heat and allow to steep
with the lid on for 30 minutes.
Serve and enjoy!*

•

The feeling of being around the fire at eleven o'clock on Christmas night with your beautiful family is The Ten of Cups. You're exhausted from all the work you've put in to make the holiday perfect, but all that effort made this moment possible. If you feel like this evening couldn't get any better, pour yourself some of this mulled wine and let it make the moment even sweeter.

THE PAGE OF CUPS

Rim a glass with sugar and then add the following to a cocktail shaker:

Ice
2 shots vodka
2 shots cranberry juice
2 shots grapefruit juice
Shake and serve in your rimmed glass with a lime wedge

•

If you've ever been to a bar in your early twenties, you've definitely witnessed a good-looking young man with buckets of charm, but teaspoons of maturity waltz up to a girl and offer her a drink. We'll bet you nine times out of ten, he bought her a Seabreeze. This pretty pink glass is brimming with vodka and lost inhibitions. For many, it contains both the fond memories of youthful dalliances and a sickening reminder of mistakes made in the name of experience.

THE KNIGHT OF CUPS

Rim a glass with salt, and then add the following to a cocktail shaker:

Ice
3 shots grapefruit juice
2 shots tequila
1 shot triple sec
1 shot agave
Shake and serve over ice

•

The Knight of Cups indicates that a romantic offer is in your midst. This knight is the most emotionally available and mature of all his counterparts, and he is also the most romantically inclined. Be prepared to catch feelings because you most likely will! This grapefruit margarita will be the perfect drink to share with your best friend as you tell them all about the juicy details of this new love interest.

THE QUEEN OF CUPS

Pour the following into a glass:

2 shots gin
1 shot rose simple syrup
1 shot lemon juice
Top with sparkling rosé

•

The Queen of Cups is one of those people who has an incredible emotional capacity but often chooses not to show it. She does this to protect herself and maintain life's upper hand. If you naturally feel everything—and I mean everything—this intensely, you may find that being closed off to most of the world is the only way to survive. The Queen of Cups knows how to be the kindest person you'll ever meet while also having the capacity to be the toughest. This rosé French 75 is subtly strong and full of nuance, the perfect thing to sip while you ponder if anyone will ever be capable of loving you the way you love them.

THE KING OF CUPS

**Rim a glass with salt and add the following
to a cocktail shaker:**

Ice
1/2 shot lime juice
1/2 shot simple syrup
1 shot limoncello
1 shot gin
Shake and pour into your rimmed glass over ice
Top off with soda water and garnish with a lime twist

·

The King of Cups is solid, mature, and patient; he is compassionate but does not always wear his heart on his sleeve. This refreshing cocktail is the perfect way to either help get into the mindset of The King of Cups yourself or to celebrate this person in your life. This drink, like the card, is both potent and understated. It is a drink best suited to an afternoon on the veranda or an evening out at the bar enjoying the summer night.

ABOUT THE AUTHORS

Homegrown in Willits, California, Rose grew up on her parents' sustainable mini-farm, growing veggies, running barefoot, and eating a little dirt along the way.

Emma grew up on the California-Nevada border in a town of 329 people amongst a sea of Redneck-Hippies (yes, they exist, and we love them).

After a few years of tangential interactions at Hampshire College, they found each other and became close friends, bonded by a love of art, life, and the occult. Together they muddled their way through a slightly liquor-fueled haze of youthful transgressions and memory-worthy late-night shenanigans. Literally one for the books.